Ruth

Drawing on a Deeper Love

A six-session Bible study for individuals and small groups

By Mark Greene

licc.

*'May the LORD repay you
for what you have done.
May you be richly rewarded
by the LORD, the God of Israel,
under whose wings you
have come to take refuge.'*

Boaz to Ruth, Ruth 2:12

INTER-VARSITY PRESS
36 Causton Street, London SW1P 4ST, England
Email: ivp@ivpbooks.com
Website: www.ivpbooks.com

Mark Greene has asserted his right under the Copyright, Designs
and Patents Act, 1988, to be identified as Author of this work.

First published 2020

British Library Cataloguing-in-Publication Data
A catalogue record for this book is available from the British Library

ISBN: 978-1-78974-162-9
eBook ISBN: 9781789742251

Typeset in Great Britain by Sublime
Printed in Great Britain by Ashford Colour Press Ltd., Gosport, Hampshire

Inter-Varsity Press publishes Christian books that are true to the
Bible and that communicate the gospel, develop discipleship
and strengthen the church for its mission in the world.

IVP originated within the Inter-Varsity Fellowship, now the
Universities and Colleges Christian Fellowship, a student movement
connecting Christian Unions in universities and colleges throughout
Great Britain, and a member movement of the International
Fellowship of Evangelical Students. Website: www.uccf.org.uk.
That historic association is maintained, and all senior IVP staff
and committee members subscribe to the UCCF Basis of Faith.

Contents

Features

The Gateway Seven

Exodus Law

Ezekiel Prophecy

Mark Gospel

1 Peter Letters

Proverbs Wisdom

Revelation Apocalyptic

Ruth Narrative

The Gateway Seven Bible Study Series

We don't approach a novel in the same way we tackle a legal document. We don't read poetry in the same way we might read a letter from a friend. So, we don't read the 66 books of the Bible as if they were all the same kind of writing. Story, song, law, letter, and more, all make up the rich repository of writing that together is God's word to us.

For *The Gateway Seven* series we've selected seven books of the Bible that each represent a different kind of writing. The mini-features sprinkled through the studies, together with the questions suggested for discussion, invite you to explore each book afresh in a way that's sensitive to its genre as well as to the concerns of the book itself.

Each study engages with a different kind of writing. However, each one in the series has been crafted with the same central desire: to offer a gateway to a deeper love of God's word and richer insights into its extraordinary implications for all of life, Monday through Sunday.

'May your kingdom come – on earth as in heaven', Jesus taught us to pray. May your kingdom come in our homes and places of work and service. May your kingdom come at the school gate as well as in the sanctuary. May your kingdom come in the hydrotherapy pool, in the council chamber, on the estate, around the Board table. May your kingdom come as we learn to live our everyday lives as beloved sons and daughters, wondrously wrapped up in our Father's 'family business'.

Our prayer is that these seven distinctive books of the Bible will be a gateway for you to a richer, deeper, transforming life with God wherever you are – seven days a week.

Tracy Cotterell
The Gateway Seven Series Editor
Managing Director - Mission, LICC

Prologue

Drawing on a Deeper Love

Ruth is one of those books whose riches never seem to run out. You can read it in ten minutes and relish it for a lifetime.

On the surface, it's a simple and very short story about two ordinary, Iron Age widows trying to find a way forward in a spiritually decaying culture, and in an agonising, potentially crushing mix of famine, poverty, barrenness, displacement, migration, sexual threat, exclusion, sexism, racism, grief.

It's also a story about how two of the most remarkable and lauded people in the entire Bible cross racial, economic, and ethnic barriers and come to be married. And it's also the story of how a Moabite widow becomes the matriarch of the monarchical line that will not only lead to King David but to King Jesus himself.

At a deeper level this is a book about self-giving love in action – *chesed* in the original Hebrew, where the 'ch' is pronounced like the 'ch' in the Scottish 'loch'. *Chesed* is sometimes translated 'kindness', sometimes 'loving kindness', 'mercy', 'love', 'compassion'. The word appears three times in Ruth (1:8; 2:20; 3:10) but as a concept it is the fuel of the plot and the distinctive characteristic of Ruth, of Boaz, to a lesser extent of Naomi, and vitally of God himself. Indeed, in the Psalms, it's often applied to God, for example in Psalm 136, where the refrain 'his *chesed* (love) endures forever' reveals the wide range of ways that God expresses his love.

Chesed, like 'grace' in English, carries the connotation of a generosity that does not relate to the merit of the recipient. It's the love that doesn't have to, but does.

God after all doesn't have to carry on showing us mercy, doesn't have to carry on forgiving us, doesn't have to send us his son to give his life that we might have life eternal. The word suggests the kind of love that goes beyond social convention or even the requirements of the law. God's love, however, is very definitely expressed through his laws, as Jesus makes clear:

> '"Love the Lord your God with all your heart and with all your soul and with all your mind." This is the first and greatest commandment. And the second is like it: "Love your neighbour as yourself." All the Law and the Prophets hang on these two commandments.'
>
> Matthew 22:37–40

The whole teaching of Moses and all the prophetic writings are an expression of God's love, all intended to help us see how to love him and love our neighbour.

So, for example, the God of love instituted the law of gleaning because he anticipated that there would be people so destitute that they wouldn't have any other legal way to feed themselves. However, the law of gleaning doesn't capture the full extent of God's love for the poor, nor seek to limit the scope of our response, as we will see in Ruth 2. The God of love certainly wants more for those created in his image than that we should merely survive. And to love God is to seek to understand and want what he wants, and to love as he loves.

Chesed then includes, but goes beyond, the love that an ordinarily kind person might show. At its richest, it's a quality of love that if someone didn't extend it to you, you wouldn't raise an eyebrow, or feel offended. In fact, you might not notice. Orpah does no wrong by following Naomi's instruction and returning to her family. But when someone shows you *chesed*, it makes you gasp, stops you in your tracks, renders you speechless... and then turns you to praise.

As we shall see, Ruth is indeed an ordinary woman from an unnamed town and a scorned nation. But the quality of her self-giving love not only evokes wonder and astonishment from the people she encounters but an extraordinary

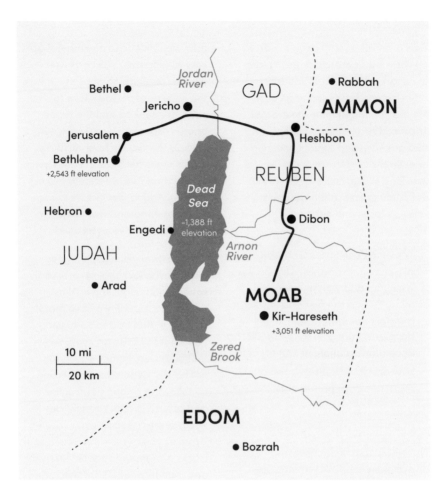

level of blessing from the Lord of *Chesed* himself. Her actions, it seems, are drawn from the well of a deeper love that foreshadows the perfect expression of that deeper love in the self-giving of her descendant – Christ, the lamb of God.

Ruth's example is made all the more remarkable and compelling precisely because she is an ordinary woman, just a peasant. It's a reminder to us all that our ever-so-ordinary Christian life of work, family, relationships, community has a distinctive part to play in God's epic purposes in time and eternity. And so it does.

About the writing of Ruth

We know that the events in the book happened between 1200 and 1075 BC but not precisely when. But we don't know who wrote the book, or indeed when between around 1000 BC and 400 BC it was written. That encourages us to consider the story as we have it, rather than reading back into it from the known concerns of a later period. So, we know it was written after David was crowned king, but we don't know if it was written in his reign, as some scholars think, in Solomon's reign, as others do, or much later to engage with the question of mixed marriages that was so significant in the time of Ezra and Nehemiah. It's not clear. And it's testimony to the skill of the writer that the story doesn't seem to have a particular agenda, even though it clearly has much to teach us.

The book is structured round a series of choices that the characters face and resolve in four conversations:

Naomi, Ruth, and Orpah on the road to Bethlehem – chapter 1
Boaz and Ruth at work on an ordinary day – chapter 2
Boaz alone at night with Ruth at the threshing floor – chapter 3
Ruth's closest guardian-redeemer and Boaz at the city gate – chapter 4

Like the people in this story, we too may find ourselves in situations where we have choices to make and don't have the luxury of pressing 'pause' to go pray and ponder. How will we choose? And what will our choices reveal about our character, our priorities, and our understanding of God's character and his priorities?

May your study of Ruth
strengthen your trust in the Lord,
fill you with wonder at his gracious ways,
and help you to draw more deeply
from the well of his unfathomable love.

Shalom, shalom,
Mark Greene

Making the Most of Ruth

Studying Ruth

This study explores the book over six sessions, chapter by chapter
for the first four. Then we look back over the book again. How might
the book's conclusion enrich our understanding of earlier passages,
not least the very first verse? What patterns can we now see in the
book overall? What are the implications of those patterns for our
understanding of the book, the characters, God's purposes, and our
own lives today?

Session 1 | Loving in Terrible Times (Ruth 1)

Session 2 | Loving at Work (Ruth 2)

Session 3 | Loving through Risk (Ruth 3)

Session 4 | Loving beyond Imagination (Ruth 4)

Session 5 | The Loving God at Work (Ruth 1–4)

Session 6 | The Loving God through History (Ruth 1–4)

You can work through each session on your
own, one-to-one, or in a small group.

If your church is covering the book of Ruth in a sermon series, this
study is a really helpful way to deepen your understanding of the book
and explore its implications for Monday to Saturday life. And working
in a group is an opportunity to encourage one another with insights
and stories of how people have seen God at work in their own context.

Each group has its own way of doing things, so the
session plan is a suggestion, not a rule.

Suggested session plan

_____

1 Pray to open

2 Read the 'First Thoughts' section

3 Read the Bible passage

4 Work through the questions

They cover the session's main theme, what the
Bible passage says and means, going deeper,
and living out the passage. Many questions don't
have 'right' or 'wrong' answers. Naturally, group
leaders may want to pick out the most pertinent
questions for their group, or add their own.

5 Pray to close

Don't feel bound by the prayer prompts.
If your study has taken a different direction,
be flexible in responding to each other's needs.

You'll see that we've included five brief features on questions or
issues related to the background and study of the book of Ruth.
Together with some real-life stories – lived examples of how God's
word can be worked out in daily life – we hope they will help to
deepen your understanding of the book and its implications.

We've changed the names of the people in the stories
and some details to preserve their anonymity.

Participating in the study

—

Before each session, you might like to read the passage together with one of the features, and any explanation boxes or stories that accompany the session. After you meet, you might like to pursue some of the 'Going Deeper' questions on your own.

Before the first session

Ruth is a short book, so take a moment to read it through in one go, perhaps simply noting down the things that strike you.

Ruth – An Old Testament Reading Plan

—

Ruth is rich in allusion to other sections of the Old Testament. You can get ready to read Ruth by using a twenty-day reading plan which will immerse you in the biblical material that the original readers would have been familiar with. There's usually a question or two for each reading to help you focus on some aspect of the passage that is particularly pertinent to Ruth.

Download at licc.org.uk/ruth

My frontline

Your frontline is an everyday place where you live, work, study, or play and where you're likely to connect with people who aren't Christians. Before you start the study, reflect on your frontline using these questions.

Where is your frontline?

What do you do there?

Who's there?

What's going on at the moment?

What are you excited about or struggling with?

What opportunities for making an impact for Christ do you see in and through what you do and who you connect with?

Come back to this reflection throughout the sessions, praying and trusting that God will direct your ways through his word.

Reading Old Testament narrative – part one

Every culture tells their stories differently. Old Testament narratives are no exception and are written in a very different way from the way contemporary Western writers tell stories – true or fictional.

In Old Testament stories there is much less description of people and places, and much less detail about what people are thinking or feeling than in Western fiction or historiography. In Jane Austen's *Pride and Prejudice*, for example, we know a fair amount about what Mr Darcy's estate looks like, 'The park was very large, and contained great variety of ground'. We know that the house 'was a large, handsome stone building' and that 'the rooms were lofty and handsome, and their furniture ... neither gaudy nor uselessly fine'. Similarly, we're told quite a lot about what Elizabeth Bennet is thinking, that she was 'overpowered by shame and vexation', or 'enraged against herself for being so silly'. The same interest in detail applies to, for example, a contemporary newspaper report on anything from a football match to a natural disaster: we're given quite a bit of information about the events, the people involved, and the implications of what happened. By contrast, how much do we know about what is going on in Abraham's mind as he walks towards Mount Moriah preparing to sacrifice his son (Genesis 22)?

Nothing.

Similarly, Old Testament narrative makes sparing use of adjectives and adverbial expressions. So, for example, people speak, may shout, or occasionally whisper but you won't find much description of *how* they might have said the words – 'sarcastically,' 'with a lilt in her voice', or 'with furrowed brow'. The writing is pared back. Still, although there is much less detail, the detail we are given matters a great deal. And we often have to slow down to allow the full force of the material to have its impact. Indeed, the book of Ruth cannot really be appreciated unless we recognise the terrible emotional and economic implications of the loss that the characters suffer in the opening chapter.

Old Testament narrative creates much of its impact by the very careful choice of vocabulary to generate thematic connections both within the story itself and to other parts of the Old Testament. These connections are made through the repetition of words or phrases, or through plays on words, or through the deliberate use of words that sound similar. In Ruth, look out, for example, for how the writer works with ideas about 'empty' and 'full', not only in the words used but in the choice of the situations described. In sum, we're meant to read a biblical story like Ruth with a greater alertness to individual words than in a contemporary novel.

We are invited to wonder, to ponder.

Indeed, Old Testament narratives are descriptive not prescriptive. They tell us what happened, not what should have happened. Often, as in Ruth, the actions of the characters resist easy interpretation or rapid reduction to teaching points. Rather, precisely because we are given a story, rather than laws, we are invited to engage imaginatively, prayerfully, patiently in the drama as it unfolds. It's similar to the way we might get to the end of an episode in a TV soap and wonder: why did they do that? What will happen next? Will he? Will she? In the case of Ruth, we're meant to stop and wonder where God was in the famine and the deaths of the three husbands, or why on earth Naomi sent her daughter-in-law to meet a man in the middle of the night in a secluded place, or what we might have done if Ruth had turned up in one of our fields. In sum, we're supposed to imagine ourselves in the shoes of the various characters, to consider how we might have responded, how *we* might feel if that had happened to us, and though centuries separate us, to make the connections with our own lives.

Of course, Ruth is part of the Old Testament and of the wider Bible, so when we come to interpret the book, we do so at three levels:

- The book's significance in and of itself

- The book's role and significance in the wider story of God's dealings with the people of Israel – from Genesis to Malachi

- The book's role and significance in the whole story of God's action from Genesis to Revelation in the light of the incarnation, crucifixion, resurrection, and ascension of Jesus the Messiah

This triple-lens approach is similar to the way historians might describe a battle. They tell us what happened. Then they look at the significance of that battle in the context of the war being fought. And then they might pull back the lens further and consider its significance in the whole history of a nation. So, for example, the Battle of Britain was a remarkable victory against overwhelming odds. It was also a victory that prevented a German invasion of Britain, altering the course of the war. And it gained a wider significance as the words of Churchill's radio broadcast seeped

into the national consciousness, 'Never in the field of human conflict was so much owed by so many to so few'. Similarly, when we read the accounts of God's dealing with his people in the Old Testament we seek to understand what he was doing at that time, how it fits with his plans for Israel, and how we are to view it in the light of the life and work of Christ.

In the case of Ruth, the book's final sentences explicitly invite us to consider the story in the light of God's ongoing purposes for Israel. But the encouragement to do so does come in the final sentences, so we need to try not to jump ahead, but to let the story speak to us along the way, not just through the lens of its finale, or the lens of Jesus' life and work.

Digging into the Context

One of the ways to stay alert to what's going on in a narrative passage is to ask the questions that journalists are trained to ask when researching a story.

Who?
Who is there? And who are they? What about the minor characters? How does their presence affect the action?

What?
What actually happens? What is said?

When?
In what era, in what year, at what time of the year, at what time of the day? After what has just happened? Before what is just about to happen?

Where?
Where do the events occur? Does the location have any significance? Imagine, for example, what you would see at the place where Naomi tries to send Ruth and Orpah away.

Why?
Why is this happening? Why do the characters say and do what they say and do?

Session 1

Loving in Terrible Times

Ruth 1

First Thoughts

'In the Blitz', 'in the 60s', 'in the Thatcher years' conjure up a host of associations in British minds. And the phrase that opens the book of Ruth would have done likewise for its original readers – 'in the days when the judges ruled'. Yes, the book of Ruth has sometimes been read as if it were a romantic country idyll, an Iron Age boy-meets-girl-from-the-wrong-side-of-the-tracks rom-com – *When Bozie met Ruthie* – but that notion is exploded by those opening words.

'The days when the judges ruled' was an era of radical moral and spiritual decline. Time and again Israel rebel against God. Divine discipline follows until the people repent and cry for help. The pattern repeats – round and down like a vortex spiralling into darkness. Though we can't be certain, the events in Ruth seem to occur after Gideon and before the time when civil war breaks out after a priest's concubine is gang-raped to death by a group of Benjaminites. At the same time, the mention of the judges reminds the reader of God's mercy and many interventions.

Like Ruth, we don't get to choose the times we're born in and how they make the joys and jolts of life easier or harder to respond to. Certainly, 'the Brexit years' in the UK are unlikely to be remembered as our 'finest hour'. In such a time as this, how do we respond in godly ways to hardship, suffering, loss – financial, relational, physical, mental? Our own? And other people's?

Read – Ruth 1 👁

—

¹ In the days when the judges ruled, there was a famine in the land. So a man from Bethlehem in Judah, together with his wife and two sons, went to live for a while in the country of Moab. ² The man's name was Elimelek, his wife's name was Naomi, and the names of his two sons were Mahlon and Kilion. They were Ephrathites from Bethlehem, Judah. And they went to Moab and lived there.

³ Now Elimelek, Naomi's husband, died, and she was left with her two sons. ⁴ They married Moabite women, one named Orpah and the other Ruth. After they had lived there about ten years, ⁵ both Mahlon and Kilion also died, and Naomi was left without her two sons and her husband.

⁶ When Naomi heard in Moab that the LORD had come to the aid of his people by providing food for them, she and her daughters-in-law prepared to return home from there. ⁷ With her two daughters-in-law she left the place where she had been living and set out on the road that would take them back to the land of Judah.

⁸ Then Naomi said to her two daughters-in-law, 'Go back, each of you, to your mother's home. May the LORD show you kindness, as you have shown kindness to your dead husbands and to me. ⁹ May the LORD grant that each of you will find rest in the home of another husband.'

Then she kissed them goodbye and they wept aloud ¹⁰ and said to her, 'We will go back with you to your people.'

¹¹ But Naomi said, 'Return home, my daughters. Why would you come with me? Am I going to have any more sons, who could become your husbands? ¹² Return home, my daughters; I am too old to have another husband. Even if I thought there

was still hope for me – even if I had a husband tonight and then gave birth to sons – ¹³ would you wait until they grew up? Would you remain unmarried for them? No, my daughters. It is more bitter for me than for you, because the LORD's hand has turned against me!'

¹⁴ At this they wept aloud again. Then Orpah kissed her mother-in-law goodbye, but Ruth clung to her.

¹⁵ 'Look,' said Naomi, 'your sister-in-law is going back to her people and her gods. Go back with her.'

¹⁶ But Ruth replied, 'Don't urge me to leave you or to turn back from you. Where you go I will go, and where you stay I will stay. Your people will be my people and your God my God. ¹⁷ Where you die I will die, and there I will be buried. May the LORD deal with me, be it ever so severely, if even death separates you and me.' ¹⁸ When Naomi realised that Ruth was determined to go with her, she stopped urging her.

¹⁹ So the two women went on until they came to Bethlehem. When they arrived in Bethlehem, the whole town was stirred because of them, and the women exclaimed, 'Can this be Naomi?'

²⁰ 'Don't call me Naomi,' she told them. 'Call me Mara, because the Almighty has made my life very bitter. ²¹ I went away full, but the LORD has brought me back empty. Why call me Naomi? The LORD has afflicted me; the Almighty has brought misfortune upon me.'

²² So Naomi returned from Moab accompanied by Ruth the Moabite, her daughter-in-law, arriving in Bethlehem as the barley harvest was beginning.

Focus on the Theme ⊕

1. Think of a time when you or someone close to you faced hardship, suffering or loss. How did you see God at work through that time?

_____

_____

_____

_____

_____

_____

_____

_____

Of Moab and Moabites

The Moabites were the descendants of Abraham's nephew Lot through an incestuous union with Lot's oldest daughter (Genesis 19:30–38). They became idol-worshippers, and Israelite relations with them over the centuries had been fraught. When the people of Israel left Egypt and made their way to Canaan, the Moabites did not offer them bread and water, and their king tried to have them cursed (Numbers 24:17). Later, at Shittim, a large number of Israelite men had sex with Moabite women and worshipped their gods, leading to the plague that killed 24,000 Israelites (Numbers 25:1–9).

What Does the Bible Say? 🔖

2. Why does Naomi release, and discourage, her daughters-in-law from coming with her to Bethlehem (1:8–13)? See the feature on levirate marriage on page 28.

What does she want for them?

3. As a Moabite widow, what is Ruth risking by choosing to live in an Israelite community?

4. What do Ruth's decision and her words of commitment (1:16–17) reveal about her character and her priorities?

And what does Ruth's decision suggest about Naomi's witness to her over the years?

5. What do Naomi's words in Moab (1:8–15) and on arriving in Bethlehem (1:20–21) reveal about her character and her emotional and spiritual state?

Levirate marriage

When Naomi tells Orpah and Ruth that she is too old to have another son to become one of their husbands, she is referring to the law of levirate marriage (Deuteronomy 25:5 –10). If a man dies without an heir then his brother has an obligation to marry his widow to ensure there is a child to carry on the dead man's name. This is still practised in a number of countries today. In contexts where there is no welfare state and no possibility of saving for the equivalent of a pension, the practice not only preserves the name of the deceased but, vitally, ensures that the widow has a child to provide for her in old age.

Going Deeper

6. Famines occur frequently in the Old Testament. Sometimes it's clear God is using them to discipline his people (Deuteronomy 32:18-24; Judges 6:1-6; 2 Samuel 21:1), sometimes they just happen (Genesis 12:1). Compare how, in response to famine, Abraham decides to go down to Egypt (Genesis 12:10) with how his grandson Jacob does (Genesis 45:27 – 46:4). How might this background help us discern how we are to view Elimelek's decision to move to Moab (1:1)?

7. Naomi and Elimelek move to Moab to find food and their sons marry Moabite women. How might the history of Israel's relations with Moab help us discern whether God might have approved or disapproved of these decisions?

Living it Out ((o))

8. Is there a godly character quality you've noticed in Ruth or Naomi that you'd like to grow in?

9. 'In the days when the judges ruled' (1:1) gives the reader an indication of Israel's culture at the time. How would you describe the culture of your frontline (a place you regularly spend time with people who don't know Jesus)?

What is positive?
What is challenging?

10. Is there someone you know to be in crisis?

How might you come alongside them?

Responding in Prayer ♛

- Pray for the specific character quality you want to grow in.

- Is there someone you particularly yearn to hear say the words, 'Your God will be my God'? Name them to one another and pray for their salvation.

- Pray for the person you were thinking about in question 10.

What's in a name?

Names are often highly significant in Old Testament culture, capturing some aspect of the person's character or their family's history. For example, the names that Leah gives her sons track her emotional and spiritual state at each birth: from Reuben (sounds like 'he has seen my misery' and means 'see, a son') to Judah ('praise') (Genesis 29:31–35).

From Genesis 1:5 on, God is presented as the God who names, and, by doing so, assigns value to objects as well as to people. He then graciously delegates to human beings the overall task of developing language, and distinguishing one creature and one person from another (Genesis 2:19, 23). Nevertheless, sometimes God names people himself or tells a parent what to name them. Hosea, for example, is told to name his first daughter Lo-Ruhamah, meaning 'not loved', to signify his decision not to show love to Israel (Hosea 1:6–7). In the New Testament, Elizabeth and Zechariah are instructed by the angel to name their child John (Luke 1:13) – 'the Lord gives'.

Sometimes God renames people himself: Abram becomes Abraham (from 'exalted father' to 'father of many') (Genesis 17:5); Sarai becomes Sarah (from, debatably, 'she who strives' to 'princess') (Genesis 17:15). And we see Jesus doing the same thing: Simon becomes Peter, 'rock', for 'on this rock I will build my church' (Matthew 16:18). And James and John are Boanerges, 'sons of thunder' (Mark 3:17).

Here in Ruth the names are also significant and would have carried connotations for the Hebrew reader that in a few cases we can't be sure of. And the book itself draws our attention to their importance when it records Naomi renaming herself Mara (1:20). In some cases, the significance of the name is obvious – Elimelek means 'my God is king'. In some cases, as with Mahlon and Kilion, the connotation is in the sound of the words, not necessarily their actual root meaning. So, imagine a character in an English story called 'Burke'. The fact that the name probably derives from an old English word 'burh' meaning fortification or manor, or that the verb, rarely used, means to suppress or avoid an issue, may have less significance than that it sounds like 'berk'. Similarly, the connotations of the sound of Mahlon and Kilion's names strike a foreboding note.

Names in Ruth in order of
appearance – meaning
or primary connotations

Bethlehem	House/home of bread
Judah	Praise
Moab	From father
Elimelek	My God is king
Naomi	Lovely, pleasant, my pleasant one
Mahlon	Sickness
Kilion	Annihilation or completeness
Orpah	Neck
Ruth	Refreshment, satiation, comfort
Mara	Bitter
Boaz	In him is strength
Obed	One who serves, server
Jesse	Gift
David	Beloved

Session 2

Loving at Work

Ruth 2

First Thoughts

When the going gets tough, the tough, the saying goes, get going. Sometimes the only thing to do in tough times is *something*, even if that something is unlikely to solve the big problem. Ruth and Naomi have nothing to eat. Without land, without apparent support from the Bethlehem community, Ruth, as we'll read, takes the only step open to her. And it's a step down economically and socially from being a daughter in her mother's house in her own country. She goes out looking for a field to glean in. She's proactive.

Of course, sometimes – or usually, for some of us – the going isn't tough, the going is fine. Or at least pretty good, so good that we perhaps don't notice that new person at the club, that new mum at the school gate, that new intern in IT. Or perhaps we have stopped noticing that long-standing member at the club that not many people talk to, that mum with worn-out shoes who always scuttles away with her head down, that middle manager who always eats lunch alone. We're fine. We don't need a new friend, or an awkward friend. We're fine. We don't need to be proactive. For our own sake, at least...

Read – Ruth 2

¹ Now Naomi had a relative on her husband's side, a man of standing from the clan of Elimelek, whose name was Boaz.

² And Ruth the Moabite said to Naomi, 'Let me go to the fields and pick up the leftover grain behind anyone in whose eyes I find favour.'

Naomi said to her, 'Go ahead, my daughter.' ³ So she went out, entered a field and began to glean behind the harvesters. As it turned out, she was working in a field belonging to Boaz, who was from the clan of Elimelek.

⁴ Just then Boaz arrived from Bethlehem and greeted the harvesters, 'The LORD be with you!'

'The LORD bless you!' they answered.

⁵ Boaz asked the overseer of his harvesters, 'Who does that young woman belong to?'

⁶ The overseer replied, 'She is the Moabite who came back from Moab with Naomi. ⁷ She said, "Please let me glean and gather among the sheaves behind the harvesters." She came into the field and has remained here from morning till now, except for a short rest in the shelter.'

⁸ So Boaz said to Ruth, 'My daughter, listen to me. Don't go and glean in another field and don't go away from here. Stay here with the women who work for me. ⁹ Watch the field where the men are harvesting, and follow along after the women. I have told the men not to lay a hand on you. And whenever you are thirsty, go and get a drink from the water jars the men have filled.'

¹⁰ At this, she bowed down with her face to the ground. She asked him, 'Why have I found such favour in your eyes that you notice me – a foreigner?'

¹¹ Boaz replied, 'I've been told all about what you have done for your mother-in-law since the death of your husband – how you left your father and mother and your homeland and came to live with a people you did not know before. ¹² May the LORD repay you for what you have done. May you be richly rewarded by the LORD, the God of Israel, under whose wings you have come to take refuge.'

¹³ 'May I continue to find favour in your eyes, my lord,' she said. 'You have put me at ease by speaking kindly to your servant – though I do not have the standing of one of your servants.'

¹⁴ At mealtime Boaz said to her, 'Come over here. Have some bread and dip it in the wine vinegar.'

When she sat down with the harvesters, he offered her some roasted grain. She ate all she wanted and had some left over. ¹⁵ As she got up to glean, Boaz gave orders to his men, 'Let her gather among the sheaves and don't reprimand her. ¹⁶ Even pull out some stalks for her from the bundles and leave them for her to pick up, and don't rebuke her.'

¹⁷ So Ruth gleaned in the field until evening. Then she threshed the barley she had gathered, and it amounted to about an ephah. ¹⁸ She carried it back to town, and her mother-in-law saw how much she had gathered. Ruth also brought out and gave her what she had left over after she had eaten enough.

¹⁹ Her mother-in-law asked her, 'Where did you glean today? Where did you work? Blessed be the man who took notice of you!'

Then Ruth told her mother-in-law about the one at whose place she had been working. 'The name of the man I worked with today is Boaz,' she said.

²⁰ 'The Lord bless him!' Naomi said to her daughter-in-law. 'He has not stopped showing his kindness to the living and the dead.' She added, 'That man is our close relative; he is one of our guardian-redeemers.'

²¹ Then Ruth the Moabite said, 'He even said to me, "Stay with my workers until they finish harvesting all my grain."'

²² Naomi said to Ruth her daughter-in-law, 'It will be good for you, my daughter, to go with the women who work for him, because in someone else's field you might be harmed.'

²³ So Ruth stayed close to the women of Boaz to glean until the barley and wheat harvests were finished. And she lived with her mother-in-law.

Picking up on gleaning

God instituted several laws to ensure that the poor, whether Israelite or resident aliens, would not starve, and could contribute to feeding themselves. With that in mind, he instructed farmers not to harvest right up to the edge of their fields, nor to go over a vineyard a second time (Leviticus 19:9), nor to pick up the grains that fell from stalks as they were being harvested. Rather, they were to leave them for the poor to glean (Leviticus 23:22). Gleaning was back-breaking work, but a steady worker might pick up a litre or more of grain a day.

Focus on the Theme

1. Think about your frontline – where you spend time in an ordinary week. In what ways do you currently seek the wellbeing of that place and the people there?

2. What significance do you see in the phrases 'As it turned out' (2:3) and 'Just then Boaz arrived' (2:4)?

3. What can we learn about Ruth's character from her actions and words in this chapter (for example: 2:2, 10, 13, 17–18)?

4. List the things that Boaz does for Ruth (for example: 2:8–9, 11–12, 14, 15–16). In what ways does Boaz go above and beyond what the law of gleaning required?

5. Boaz is not expecting Ruth to come to his field, so he's not had time to prepare. What do his actions and words reveal about his character and about the culture of the time?

What are the reasons for the actions he takes? See 2:11.

A word about a word

In Ruth 2:1, Boaz is described as 'a man of standing'. In other translations it's 'a man of renown', 'of noble character', of 'valour'. The Hebrew word is *chail* and is most frequently applied to soldiers – David's mighty men of *chail* (1 Chronicles 28:1). As such, it has connotations of heroism, but essentially it's a word about character, and it's a high accolade. Boaz uses it to describe Ruth (3:11), and those at the city gate pray that Boaz would be a doer of *chail* (4:11). Biblical heroism is not just manifested in war but in godly character and action in ordinary life.

Importantly, it sums up the woman of 'noble character' in Proverbs 31:10, whose fear of the Lord is expressed in generous, wise living in everything from household management to international trading, from childcare to care for the poor. If Proverbs shows us *chail* expressed in an exemplary way in an upper-class, wealthy woman, the book of Ruth reveals what it looks like in a poor immigrant widow and a moderately well-to-do farmer.

The guardian-redeemer

The land allocated to a
family during the distribution
of territory under Moses
and Joshua was intended
to be held by that family in
perpetuity. In an agricultural
economy, land was critical to
economic prosperity and it
was God's intention that no
family should be subjected to
multi-generational poverty.
However, if, for economic
reasons, the family needed to
sell the land, the new owner
was obliged to return it to
the original owners in the
year of Jubilee, or to sell it
to a relative of the original
family if they were seeking
to buy it back (redeem it) on
behalf of the original family.
Indeed, it was the clearly
designated responsibility
of the closest relative of
the impoverished family
– the guardian-redeemer
– to do so (see Leviticus 25,
particularly 25:25–28).

Going Deeper 🔍

6. The passage describes Ruth's first
day at work in Bethlehem. What do
we learn about her from the way
she works? See 2:2–3, 7, 17–18.

7. An ephah (2:17) is 22 litres, roughly
297,968 grains of barley. How
might the harvesters' participation
in being generous have changed
their attitudes to Ruth and Boaz?

Living it Out 🔊

8. Boaz takes several actions to bless Ruth. He prays, praises, protects, even changes the way work is done in his field. Thinking about where you are – work, club, school gate or elsewhere – what might you do to contribute to making it a better place for people to flourish?

9. Women have been oppressed in societies throughout history. What have you noticed in your context?

If you are a woman, what do you experience?

How might you respond, whatever your gender, in however small a way?

10. Boaz affirms Ruth for her kindness to Naomi. Is there someone you know who needs your kindness right now?

What will you do?

Responding in Prayer

- Thank God for the kindness you've experienced from others in recent weeks.

- Ask God for his wisdom to contribute to the *shalom* – the wholeness and peace – of your frontline, and those there.

- Pray blessing on those who, for whatever reason, are outsiders on your frontline.

ANDREW'S STORY

It's a small company on the outskirts of the city. Around
seventy people work there. They make fans, industrial
fans, not all big but all of them fans that go and go and
go. I'm sitting in the canteen waiting to see Andrew.
One of the maintenance staff is filling up the coffee
machine. Lots of offices give you coffee for free but
that's rare in factories. Here it costs 10p. 'Yeah', says
the man, 'it's a good deal and we send all the profit
to a local charity.' There's appreciation in his voice.

Later Andrew walks me round the factory. There are
gleaming twirls of silver metal all over the floor of the
machine room – shavings from the blades. You might
expect them to sweep them up and take them to the
local scrap metal merchant. And they do. You might
expect the merchant to weigh them and give them a
cheque. He does. You might expect them to pop the
cheque in the bank. They don't. They send it to a local
charity. You can't really let people into a factory to
glean but that doesn't mean you can't give the proceeds
of the gleanings to people who need some help.

It's not much, you might say. But Andrew had to
change the way they did things to make it happen.

Later he tells me about a man they caught stealing. He'd
stolen around £10,000 worth of materials. And it had
been going on a while. A good worker. But a thief. You'd
expect Andrew to do one or both of two things: hand him
over to the police and fire him. Andrew did neither.

Coffee, twirls and the thief that got away

Andrew invited him to his office and asked him why he was stealing. The man had acquired a gambling habit and the pressures that often go with it. So, Andrew did a deal with him: you go to Gamblers Anonymous, stay accountable to us and to your wife, and pay us back through your pay cheque over the next three years.

Now you might expect Andrew to ask him to pay back £10,000. Which would be fair enough surely. But Andrew asked the man how much money he'd got for the £10,000 worth of stolen goods. Around £1,500. So that was what he paid back. No point in putting pressure on a man who's already under financial pressure.

Of course, Andrew doesn't have to do any of those things. Or give a percentage of any profit they make to charitable causes – and they don't always make a profit. And he doesn't have to do any of the other little things that he does do in the field that the Lord has given him to steward, among the workers who come to work for him. He doesn't have to. But grace is in him like a river... things just flow that way.

Ruth, Judges, and the (mis)treatment of women

In the beginning, the Bible declares, men and women were both created in the image of God (Genesis 1:27). Tragically, after Adam and Eve sin, the Bible records how every society then diminishes, oppresses, and exploits women in a myriad of sulphuric ways.

This continues today, not only in countries where 'girl babies' are less desired than 'boy babies', and are aborted or killed after birth, not only in countries where domestic violence against women is a cultural assumption, but also in the UK. Indeed, whatever our laudable progress in law, academic achievement, or employment opportunity, misogyny and sexism have been experienced by almost every woman I've ever met: on the street, in the office, in our schools.

God sees it all as clearly as he saw Hagar's plight (Genesis 16:6-15).

This is not the way he intended it to be, and not the way he intends it to be. You only have to look at the way Jesus honours women or to ponder Paul's words that in Christ 'there is no male or female' (Galatians 3:20) to see that.

Certainly, the Bible gives us many examples of impressive women of God. In Judges alone there is Aksah – forthright in initiative (1:12-15); Deborah – excellent in leadership (chapters 4-5); and Samson's mother – deep in theological insight (chapter 13). Importantly, the Bible does not shy away from recording the ways women are mistreated. Again, in Judges we read of terrible violence: the human sacrifice of Jephthah's daughter (11:29-40), the gang rape of the Levite's concubine (19:25-29), the kidnapping and forced marriage of the daughters of Shiloh (21:20-23). Yes, in Ruth we see how a woman of great love, bold initiative, and verbal brilliance can resolve a desperate situation. But her actions were only necessary because the men of Bethlehem failed to take the initiative to fulfil God's laws to care for the widow and the alien, or to ensure that a guardian-redeemer stepped up to buy Naomi's land. Risky female initiative was required to generate appropriate male response. The story ends joyously for Ruth and Naomi (Ruth 4:13-17) but they still find themselves in a patriarchal society where their well-being is essentially dependent on men. Society had not changed.

In Boaz, we also begin to see a better way forward for men. When Ruth arrives in his field, he's not content to see if Ruth can cope with the predatory men around her, nor content to wait until something terrible happens to her before acting. He takes the initiative to prevent the men molesting Ruth. And he not only tells them, but he also tells Ruth that he's done it. Similarly, women in our society need to *be* safe and they need to *feel* safe. This highlights the reality that if we are to see a significant change in the way women are treated, it doesn't just fall to women to call out bad behaviour, off-colour comments, unequal treatment, and so on. It falls to men too. In the world and in the church.

The reality is, whatever our personal convictions about the roles of men and women in leadership in the church, those should not deflect us from working to create a culture in our land, in our workplaces, and in our churches that reflects the infinite value that Christ places on women. We have a way to go.

Session 3

Loving through Risk

Ruth 3

First Thoughts

Ever been in a situation where you've felt stuck – and it really matters? You just can't get the right medical treatment for your son, or you can't make ends meet, or you keep on going for interviews and can't get a job. The system ought to work but it isn't working for you. What options are open to you?

Boaz's generous change to his harvesting practice certainly ensured that Naomi and Ruth would have had enough to eat day by day, and enough to keep them going for a while once the harvest was over. However, it was far from providing any kind of longer-term security for the widows – Ruth remains unmarried, and there is no one to preserve Elimelek's name. Yes, the covenant God of Israel had repeatedly stated his concern for the widow and the poor in general (Leviticus 25:35), but had the covenant community taken any significant steps to reflect that concern? At this point the future doesn't look particularly bright for Naomi and Ruth.

What options do these vulnerable women have? What options do oppressed, systemically disadvantaged women have when life-threatening poverty strikes? Not only in low-income countries but in Europe? Crime? Prostitution? Today in Britain there are some 64,000 female prostitutes, 41% from overseas. Desperate times may require desperate measures, but desperate measures usually come with dangerous risks.

Read – Ruth 3 ◉

_____

[1] One day Ruth's mother-in-law Naomi said to her, 'My daughter, I must find a home for you, where you will be well provided for. [2] Now Boaz, with whose women you have worked, is a relative of ours. Tonight he will be winnowing barley on the threshing-floor. [3] Wash, put on perfume, and get dressed in your best clothes. Then go down to the threshing-floor, but don't let him know you are there until he has finished eating and drinking. [4] When he lies down, note the place where he is lying. Then go and uncover his feet and lie down. He will tell you what to do.'

[5] 'I will do whatever you say,' Ruth answered. [6] So she went down to the threshing-floor and did everything her mother-in-law told her to do.

[7] When Boaz had finished eating and drinking and was in good spirits, he went over to lie down at the far end of the grain pile. Ruth approached quietly, uncovered his feet and lay down. [8] In the middle of the night something startled the man; he turned – and there was a woman lying at his feet!

[9] 'Who are you?' he asked.

'I am your servant Ruth,' she said. 'Spread the corner of your garment over me, since you are a guardian-redeemer of our family.'

[10] 'The LORD bless you, my daughter,' he replied. 'This kindness is greater than that which you showed earlier: you have not run after the younger

men, whether rich or poor. ¹¹ And now, my daughter, don't be afraid. I will do for you all you ask. All the people of my town know that you are a woman of noble character. ¹² Although it is true that I am a guardian-redeemer of our family, there is another who is more closely related than I. ¹³ Stay here for the night, and in the morning if he wants to do his duty as your guardian-redeemer, good; let him redeem you. But if he is not willing, as surely as the LORD lives I will do it. Lie here until morning.'

¹⁴ So she lay at his feet until morning, but got up before anyone could be recognised; and he said, 'No one must know that a woman came to the threshing-floor.'

¹⁵ He also said, 'Bring me the shawl you are wearing and hold it out.' When she did so, he poured into it six measures of barley and placed the bundle on her. Then he went back to town.

¹⁶ When Ruth came to her mother-in-law, Naomi asked, 'How did it go, my daughter?'

Then she told her everything Boaz had done for her ¹⁷ and added, 'He gave me these six measures of barley, saying, "Don't go back to your mother-in-law empty-handed."'

¹⁸ Then Naomi said, 'Wait, my daughter, until you find out what happens. For the man will not rest until the matter is settled today.'

Dangers in the night

In Ruth 3:3–8, the writer uses language that highlights the possibility of a sexual encounter between Ruth and Boaz. 'Lie down' can obviously suggest sexual availability and the word for 'feet' can be used euphemistically for sexual organs. Furthermore, threshing floors, separate as they usually were from the main part of a village, were associated with sexual immorality and prostitution (e.g. Hosea 9:1). In addition, the narrator emphasises Boaz and Ruth's gender by progressively dropping all adjectives, so that we are left with 'the man' and 'a woman' alone at night in a secluded spot. In the end, this heightening of the possibility of immorality serves to reinforce the sexual restraint and purity of both parties.

Focus on the Theme

1. Think about a time when you've been concerned that the right thing wasn't being done on your frontline, either in relation to you or to someone else. What options were open to you? What actions did you take?

What Does the Bible Say? 🔖

2. What risks does Naomi's strategy (3:1–4) expose Ruth to?

What does Naomi expect to happen?

Why might she be doing this?

3. Ruth follows Naomi's instructions to the letter (3:3, 5–7) except in one respect (3:9b). What might this reveal about Ruth's character and priorities?

And what might be the significance of her use of the word 'corner' ('wing of your robe' – 3:9), given that in Hebrew it is the same as the word 'wing' used by Boaz in 2:12?

4. Boaz says that Ruth's kindness (*chesed* in the Hebrew) exceeds 'that which you showed earlier' (3:10; cf. 2:11; 1:16–17). Why does he say this?

5. What temptations and risks do Ruth and Naomi expose Boaz to?

What do his responses reveal about his character?

Going Deeper 🔍

6. Both Ruth (3:11) and the paragon of godly wisdom that is the woman of Proverbs 31:10-31 are described as women of *chail* – noble character (See 'A word about a word' on page 37). Though different in age, social, marital, and economic status, what characteristics do the two women share? Explore, for example, Proverbs 31:12–13, 15, 25, 26–27, 30.

7. 'Redeem' first occurs as a word in Exodus 6 where God describes himself as the one who will redeem his people. What in Exodus 6:1–8 does God promise to redeem his people from, for what purpose, and with what benefits for them?

What connections do you see with the role of guardian-redeemer in Ruth?

Living it Out (((o)))

8. Have you ever been in a situation where you questioned whether to act because of the risk to your reputation? What did you do? And why?

9. In 3:9 Ruth essentially challenges Boaz to become the answer to his own prayer of 2:12. Is there something you've been praying for that God might want you to do something to help bring about?

10. What situations do you currently find yourself in that are potentially compromising? Being away overnight for work; going to parties where there's plenty of alcohol, and perhaps drugs; engaging with vulnerable people; handling funds...?

How do you protect yourself and others who might be involved?

Responding in Prayer 👑

In line with your responses
to questions 9 and 10:

- Pray for any situations people
  are facing right now that
  require wisdom and courage.

- Pray for any situations
  where God has prompted
  you to do something.

KIM'S STORY

It's one thing to do a favour for a friend. It's another thing to do a favour for a person we don't know, just because they happen to be a friend of a friend. We'd all like to be that kind of person, but I don't suppose many of us would like it to actually happen very often.

And so it came to pass that Kim, 24 and gainfully employed Monday to Friday, with church commitments, books she can't wait to get to and friends she likes to see, popped into the mind of one of her Christian friends as 'that kind of person'.

'There's this couple, not Christians, four doors down from us, who need someone to look after their two children, eighteen months and four, delightful kids. Just for a few evenings in the summer. And we can't, what with ours and all? Could you?'

Now, Kim doesn't really like children, unless they belong to people in her own family. And babysitting is an activity that would sit alongside potholing and watching re-runs of *Coronation Street* as her idea of a good evening. But she happened to be free, so she agreed.

Kim quickly discovered that the couple could hardly bear to be in the same room together. However, later that summer they announced they were going for couples counselling for six weeks. Could Kim help out? 'Happy to', came the reply. Which was both totally true and not really true at all. It was something she could do, and whenever she thought about not doing it, she just felt selfish, and she was pretty sure God wanted her to do it, though she'd be late for her church group.

On the first night of the new six-week season the children were a nightmare, each managing to scream for a solid hour. By the end of the first evening, potholing while watching re-runs of *Coronation Street* seemed like a pretty compelling option.

A gift from a woman who doesn't like children

At the end of the sixth week, the kids had calmed down, the counselling was helping, and the couple were going to carry on for an unspecified period. 'Can you help?' the text asked. Kim prayed about it, and said she would until Christmas.

And so she did, and continued on beyond Christmas, and into July, praying for the couple, praying for the children, turning up, turning down dinners and parties, suppressing any fears of missing out. She didn't have to do it. But as she put it, 'What was needed was something I could offer them. All God was asking me for was something I could give.' Fairly quickly, the children came to trust her, and she came to like them too. 'I learned to love a family I would have no other reason ever to meet. And those kids got to grow up with both their parents.'

The counselling ended, but the marriage didn't. It flourished. As a parting gift the couple gave Kim a mug that was almost exactly the same as the one she always chose when she went round. Kim prays for the family every time she uses it.

So far, neither of the couple has become a Christian. And Kim still doesn't really like children. And hasn't taken up potholing. But there are joys, rich and deep, when the love of God for others flows through you in willing surrender to his will.

Session 4

Loving beyond Imagination

Ruth 4

First Thoughts

Some things take my breath away every time I think of them. The long, gentle, persevering, loving, joyful patience of that couple with a severely disabled child and then teenager and then young adult, and then...

The medical student who in the middle of that most demanding course did the three-hour there-and-back journey across London every two weeks for two years to spend the evening with a friend suffering with a severe mental health challenge... Every two weeks. Without fail. For two years.

The cheque that came in the post from a couple we weren't even related to but who knew we had to move house and who'd figured out that the size of the mortgage was going to make it tough for us for a fair while...

Those things don't just take my breath away, they're so extraordinary they evoke more than wonder and gratitude, they evoke praise, an awe that God can make people so very loving, so very generous. And they make me want God to bless them, to pray that he would... lavishly.

In the first three chapters of Ruth, we've already seen actions that evoke admiration and wonder and prayer. But deep love has a way of surprising us.

Read – Ruth 4

¹Meanwhile Boaz went up to the town gate and sat down there just as the guardian-redeemer he had mentioned came along. Boaz said, 'Come over here, my friend, and sit down.' So he went over and sat down. ² Boaz took ten of the elders of the town and said, 'Sit here,' and they did so. ³ Then he said to the guardian-redeemer, 'Naomi, who has come back from Moab, is selling the piece of land that belonged to our relative Elimelek. ⁴ I thought I should bring the matter to your attention and suggest that you buy it in the presence of these seated here and in the presence of the elders of my people. If you will redeem it, do so. But if you will not, tell me, so I will know. For no one has the right to do it except you, and I am next in line.' 'I will redeem it,' he said. ⁵ Then Boaz said, 'On the day you buy the land from Naomi, you also acquire Ruth the Moabite, the dead man's widow, in order to maintain the name of the dead with his property.' ⁶ At this, the guardian-redeemer said, 'Then I cannot redeem it because I might endanger my own estate. You redeem it yourself. I cannot do it.' ⁷ (Now in earlier times in Israel, for the redemption and transfer of property to become final, one party took off his sandal and gave it to the other. This was the method of legalising transactions in Israel.) ⁸ So the guardian-redeemer said to Boaz, 'Buy it yourself.' And he removed his sandal.

⁹ Then Boaz announced to the elders and all the people, 'Today you are witnesses that I have bought from Naomi all the property of Elimelek, Kilion and Mahlon. ¹⁰ I have also acquired Ruth the Moabite, Mahlon's widow, as my wife, in order to maintain the name of the dead with his property, so that his name will not disappear from among his family or from his home town. Today you are witnesses!'

[11] Then the elders and all the people at the gate said, 'We are witnesses. May the LORD make the woman who is coming into your home like Rachel and Leah, who together built up the family of Israel. May you have standing in Ephrathah and be famous in Bethlehem. [12] Through the offspring the LORD gives you by this young woman, may your family be like that of Perez, whom Tamar bore to Judah.'

[13] So Boaz took Ruth and she became his wife. When he made love to her, the LORD enabled her to conceive, and she gave birth to a son. [14] The women said to Naomi: 'Praise be to the Lord, who this day has not left you without a guardian-redeemer. May he become famous throughout Israel! [15] He will renew your life and sustain you in your old age. For your daughter-in-law, who loves you and who is better to you than seven sons, has given him birth.' [16] Then Naomi took the child in her arms and cared for him. [17] The women living there said, 'Naomi has a son!' And they named him Obed. He was the father of Jesse, the father of David.

[18] This, then, is the family line of Perez:

Perez was the father of Hezron,
[19] Hezron the father of Ram,
Ram the father of Amminadab,
[20] Amminadab the father of Nahshon,
Nahshon the father of Salmon,
[21] Salmon the father of Boaz,
Boaz the father of Obed,
[22] Obed the father of Jesse,
and Jesse the father of David.

Focus on the Theme ⊕

1. Can you think of any occasions when someone has done something so kind for you or for another person that it's made you praise God for them? If so, share it with the group.

What Does the Bible Say?

2. What do we learn about Boaz's character from the way he manages the negotiations to become Ruth's guardian-redeemer (4:1–8)?

3. Ruth and Boaz seem to give their firstborn son into Naomi's care to bring him up (4:16–17). What do you think motivated such an extraordinary gift?

4. The elders and people elevate Ruth to the status of the great matriarchs of Israel (4:11). The women of the town say that she is better than seven sons to Naomi – seven being seen as the ideal number (4:14–15) (cf. 1 Samuel 2:5; Job 1:2). What prompts such remarkable accolades?

5. As well as looking forward to tell us that Obed is the grandfather of David, the book looks back to the patriarchs, setting these events in the context of the whole history of Israel (4:18–22). What does this suggest about how God works?

Going Deeper 🔍

6. The elders and all those at the gate refer to the family of Perez, whom Tamar bore to Judah (4:12). Tamar, a Canaanite, went to extraordinary lengths to preserve Judah's line. Read Genesis 38. What is similar and what is different about the two stories, and the two women (Tamar and Ruth), and the two men (Judah and Boaz)? What does the comparison serve to highlight about Ruth?

7. How might Ruth's gift of her son to Naomi (4:16–17) help us to appreciate the extraordinary nature of God's gift of his Son (John 3:16)?

From 'empty' to 'full'

What kind of role would Naomi play in her grandson's life? The combination of the startling use of the Hebrew word for 'wet nurse' in 4:16, translated here as 'cared for', and the townswomen's announcement that 'Naomi has a son' (4:17), both point to a bigger role for Naomi than 'grannie on call'. It suggests that Naomi would be acting as the child's primary carer, though, given how small Bethlehem was, inevitably close by Ruth and Boaz. This shift in the usual relationship is reinforced by the women of the town, who state that it will be Obed who will look after Naomi in her old age, rather than Ruth and Boaz. So, Naomi who came back to Bethlehem 'empty' (Ruth 1:21) now sits with her arms filled with her 'son', and a rich life to look forward to.

Lot: Remembered and Redeemed

In the first two chapters of Ruth, there is a heavy emphasis on Ruth's Moabite nationality. But in chapter 3, the events at the threshing floor recall the tribe's origins.

In Genesis 19, Lot, Abraham's nephew, and his wife and two daughters are plucked out of Sodom by a pair of angels just before the incineration of the town. Lot's wife looks back and is turned into a pillar of salt. Traumatised, Lot hunkers down in a remote cave and fails to even begin to seek husbands for his two daughters. Desperate to preserve the family line, they get him drunk and seduce him. Each bears a son. The first is Moab, meaning 'from father'.

The parallels with Ruth 3 are startling: in both accounts, an unmarried young woman, intent on preserving a family line, takes the initiative to make a nocturnal approach to an older man who has had something to drink. The reader is meant to wonder whether Ruth will seduce the older man as her ancestresses did. It is as if the scene from Genesis 19 is being replayed, but this time it's being done righteously. Still, the parallel suggests that it's not just that Ruth is being redeemed, but that Lot's line, though tainted by sin, is now folded back into the line of blessing.

This is analogous to the parallels Paul makes between the first Adam and the second Adam (Romans 5:12–21). Adam disobeyed in the garden and did his own will, rejecting the Father's will. Christ, the second Adam, obeys in the garden, choosing his Father's will, not his own, demonstrating the possibility of a perfect way, and opening it up to us all.

God had not forgotten Lot's line. Through Ruth's purity, it is reincorporated into the covenant people of God. The mistakes and sins of our parents and grandparents and great-grandparents need not be ours. The cycle can be broken.

Nothing in our past is a barrier to being folded into the purposes of God.

Living it Out

8. Ruth and Naomi's circumstances have been radically transformed since the end of chapter 1. Looking back on your own life, share an example of how God has turned a situation around.

9. Boaz stands up for Ruth's interests using his status and skills to do so. Is there someone who you might be able to help get justice?

10. The elders and people at the gate, and the women of the community, publicly acclaim the actions and character of Boaz and Ruth respectively. Is there someone, an unsung hero/heroine perhaps, on your frontline or in your church community whose character or actions you could affirm, privately or publicly – in a church service even?

Responding in Prayer

- Give thanks and pray for the 'unsung heroes/heroines' you've mentioned.

- Ask for wisdom and courage for any situation where God is calling you to get involved to seek justice or reconciliation.

Fruitfulness anticipated

In Hebrew, as in English, the word 'seed' applies both to botanical and human seed. In the NIV in 4:12, the Hebrew for 'seed' is translated 'offspring'. 'Offspring', however, misses the implication that 'seed' refers not only to the next generation but implies the capacity to create another one after that. Furthermore, Boaz's lavish gift of grain to Naomi in 3:15–17 was not merely giving her food, but symbolically promising to seek to meet her other need – for a child through Ruth.

Reading Old Testament narrative – part two

Think of any long-running TV series, or film franchise – *EastEnders* or James Bond, for example. Imagine you're a lifelong fan. You'll know all the characters, remember most of the key events, be able to recite some of the lines: 'Do you expect me to talk?' says Bond. 'No, Mr Bond,' replies Goldfinger, 'I expect you to die.'

Now when you watch the next in the series, you take all that knowledge with you. You can see how this episode relates to the others, you can instantly spot changes and inconsistencies. Often the better you know the overall franchise the richer your experience of the latest expression of it.

It is similar when we come to Old Testament stories. The better we know the Old Testament the richer our reading becomes. And this is precisely because Old Testament stories deliberately seek to create connections not only between different sections within one story but also between other stories and passages in the Bible. So, when we're reading stories in the Bible, it's helpful to listen out for echoes elsewhere in the biblical book we're reading as well as other books in the Bible.

Sometimes the connections within a book are highlighted simply through the repetition of a word. So, in 2:12, Boaz prays for Ruth to be protected by the Lord's 'wings'. Then, in 3:9, Ruth asks him to stretch the 'wing' of his garment over her. Similarly, Naomi, in chapter 1, prays that her daughters-in-law would find a 'home' – rest, ease, full contentment – through a husband. Then in chapter 3, as she begins to heal, and recover hope, and develop the capacity to take initiative, Naomi says to Ruth, 'My daughter, I must find a *home* for you, where you will be well provided for' (3:1). This internal repetition serves to alert the reader to the reality that Naomi is seeking to contribute to answering her own prayer, a prayer that in 1:11–13 she was adamant she could do nothing practical to realise.

Beyond making internal connections within a story, the narratives often seek to draw connections with other parts of the Old Testament, to help direct our interpretation, or to highlight a comparison. So, as we have seen in 4:11–12, the community's prayer raises Ruth's status to that of a matriarch. This invites us to compare Ruth with

Rachel and Leah, yes, but then also with Sarah and Rebekah. How does she compare?

Similarly, Ruth's Moabite ethnicity, and the frequent repetition of the word 'Moabite', invite the reader to engage with all the passages associated with Moab, not only those which describe their actions, but the legal passages which forbid interaction with them, and those passages in Deuteronomy, for example, which might indicate that marriage to a Moabite would be outside God's will.

This richness of allusion also applies to those passages that might point to events taking place after Ruth, firstly because Ruth may have actually been written after them, so that the writer would have been aware of them. For example, it's almost certain that the writer of Ruth knew that Jesse had eight sons, and that David was the eighth (1 Samuel 16:10–11), when he recorded the women's comment that Ruth is better to Naomi than seven sons (4:15). What is better than seven sons? Ruth. And an eighth son. Or at least an eighth son like David.

The second reason we pay attention to such passages is because even if they were written after Ruth, they may still throw light on the story. After all, it is by the Holy Spirit that all Scripture comes to us. So, for example, 300 years or so after Obed is born, Micah prophesies that the Messiah will be born in Bethlehem (Micah 5:2). We might then ask: why Bethlehem? Why not Jerusalem or Hebron? Is God honouring the extraordinary prayers of the people of that community by choosing their town as his Son's birthplace, just as he answers their prayer that Ruth would become the matriarch of a new dynasty? We see this, too, in the New Testament where we discover that Boaz is the son or grandson of Rahab, a prostitute (Matthew 1:5). And that information may serve to expand our appreciation of Boaz and his sexual restraint, and of God's gracious invitation to all people, regardless of ethnicity, religion, or moral history.

So now as we look back over the book of Ruth, what connections can we see with other passages, and how does that enrich our appreciation of Ruth and Boaz, and indeed of the way God works over time to redeem the remote as well as the recent past?

Session 5

The Loving God at Work

Ruth 1-4

First Thoughts

My family and I were 'chalet-sitting' for friends in Switzerland. The chalet had a basement accessed from outside through a very, very old door with a very, very old lock, turned by a very, very old, large, forged iron key. Now the basement had a table tennis table and one evening, my son Tomi, 8, took the key and got the basement ready for us to play. After we'd finished, he couldn't find the key. Panic soared as we searched.

It was getting late, so I suggested praying and looking again in the morning. Just then what popped into my mind was the incident in 2 Kings 6 when one of Elisha's young prophets drops a valuable, borrowed, iron axe-head into the River Jordan. The young prophet tells Elisha. And Elisha throws a stick into the Jordan and the axe-head rises to the surface. I told Tomi the story. We prayed to the God of Elisha who can find lost iron and went to bed. The following morning, I went looking for the lost key. Ten seconds later, I saw it on the cobblestone path that led to the basement door. We'd looked there several times the previous evening.

The way God acted in the young prophet's life boosted my faith to seek a similar miracle. Of course, God responds as he wills. But still, the Bible reminds us of what's possible when God gets involved.

As we reflect on what we learn about the God of Ruth and Boaz and Naomi from this book, how might it shape our living and our praying?

Focus on the Theme

1. In what ways have you seen
God act in your life? Answering
prayer? Apparent coincidences
that turn out to be significant?
Miraculous provision?

> 'So she went out, entered
> a field and began
> to glean behind the
> harvesters. As it turned
> out, she was working in a
> field belonging to Boaz,
> who was from the clan of
> Elimelek.' 2:3

> 'When Boaz had finished
> eating and drinking and
> was in good spirits, he
> went over to lie down at
> the far end of the grain
> pile. Ruth approached
> quietly, uncovered his
> feet and lay down. In
> the middle of the night
> something startled the
> man; he turned—and
> there was a woman
> lying at his feet!' 3:7-8

What Does the Bible Say?

2. There are two occasions when
we are told that God has *directly*
intervened in events in the book
of Ruth – coming to the aid of his
people by providing food for them
(1:6) and enabling Ruth to have a
son (4:13). What might the phrases
'as it turned out' and 'something
startled the man' in the verses
below teach us about how God
may also have been working?

3. There are many appeals in the
book for God to bless people.
How does God answer these three?

'Just then Boaz arrived from Bethlehem and greeted the harvesters, "The LORD be with you!" "The LORD bless you!" they answered.' 2:4–5

'Then the elders and all the people at the gate said, "We are witnesses. May the LORD make the woman who is coming into your home like Rachel and Leah, who together built up the family of Israel."' 4:11–12

'The women said to Naomi: "Praise be to the LORD, who this day has not left you without a guardian-redeemer. May he become famous throughout Israel!"' 4:14

Prayers of blessing

The book of Ruth teems with examples of people praying for God's blessing on others. There's Naomi for Ruth and Orpah (1:8–9); Boaz for his workers and his workers for him (2:4); Boaz for Ruth (2:12; 3:10); Naomi for Boaz (2:20); the elders and the people for Ruth, Boaz, and his offspring (4:11–12); and there's the townswomen for Obed (4:14). It is sometimes said that the Lord's hand is not very prominent in the book of Ruth. Yet as history unfolds, we see all these prayers of blessing, except perhaps Naomi's prayer for Orpah, being answered in glorious and surprising ways.

4. What has changed for Naomi, Ruth, and Boaz in the year or so between the end of chapter 1 and the end of chapter 4?

	Chapter 1	Chapter 4
Naomi		
Ruth		
Boaz		

5. Reflecting on your answers above, and your reading of the book so far, how would you describe the God that Ruth worships?

6. In the book of Judges, there is an overall pattern, though with variations, in the people's behaviour and in the way God works for the benefit of his people – see below.

How would you compare the way God seems to be working in the book of Ruth with the way he works in Judges?

	Judges	Ruth
Who he works with	• High profile leaders • Often flawed characters • With military prowess	
When he works	• In national crisis	
Why	• Compassion • Response to repentant prayer • Fulfil his purpose for Israel	
How	• Miraculous intervention • Supernatural empowering (e.g. Samson's strength)	

What conclusions do you draw from this?

7. How might Romans 8:28 help Naomi reflect on her life between leaving for Moab and holding Obed in her arms?

Living it Out (((o)))

8. Share a situation in your life that God radically transformed. How does it affect your attitude to any current or future challenges?

9. At first glance, it may seem God isn't particularly involved in the story of Ruth. How could you become more alert to how God is working in your life day by day?

10. The people of Bethlehem pray for Ruth and Boaz that the impact of their lives would continue for generations (4:11–12). What multi-generational prayers might you pray for your frontline, your family, your church, your town, your nation?

Responding in Prayer ♕

Pray in line with your responses to questions 9 and 10 above:

- For God to work in people you will inevitably lose touch with, or have lost touch with.

- For God to work in people or situations beyond your own lifetime.

Grace across the generations

The lists in the Old Testament of one begetter after another may seem about as exciting as watching a herd of cows walking single file through a narrow gate. Hardly worth paying attention to. These genealogies, however, are carefully designed to communicate vital truths about God and his purposes. They share several features, though with important variations.

- There's an emphasis on fathers, so when mothers are mentioned it's particularly significant.

- Most don't include every generation within the period. Rather they highlight particular people or make a particular point. For example, the important figures in some genealogies are the fifth, seventh, and tenth positions, as in the genealogy in Ruth 4:18. Matthew's genealogy is divided into three sections with 14 (2 x 7) names in each to reflect Matthew's understanding of God as a God of order, and the steady progress of his plan.

- Only the genealogy in Ruth 4 and in Genesis 5:1–32 come at the *end* of an important episode. Usually, they come before and signal that what follows is under God's blessing. Indeed, overall, genealogies are a testimony to God's faithfulness in fulfilling his covenant promises to Abraham, Isaac, and Jacob, and then on to David. He's at work in human history, and the lives of each person in the generational chain are valued and remembered – independent of whatever other contributions they may have made.

Many speculate about the purpose of the genealogy in Ruth. Some see it as a later addition to shore up David's credentials as king. However, it's simplest to see it as the affirmation of God's providential action over time and the extraordinary way that he answers the prayers of the people of Bethlehem. Ruth, after all, will become the mother of a dynasty that will shape the nation for over 600 years, as the people of God move from 'the days when the judges ruled' to a dynastic monarchy, centred round the temple in one single holy capital, Jerusalem.

BLAKE'S STORY

Blake's parents weren't people of faith, nor were his grandparents, brothers, or sister. He learned a bit about Jesus at primary school. And something stuck. And when he came to choose a secondary school, the Christian one seemed best. And he learned some more.

Blake went on to marry the daughter of deeply committed Christian parents where vibrant faith seemed to run in their families back before the foundation of the earth. About that time, passages like Deuteronomy 7:9 got him thinking:

'Know therefore that the LORD your God is God; he is the faithful God, keeping his covenant of love to a thousand generations of those who love him and keep his commandments.'

Then just after the birth of his daughter his relationship with God deepened again. And he wished that there'd been just a smidgen of spiritual commitment in the generations before him.

Our genealogies seem to matter to us, even though these days fewer of us live in the towns where we grew up, or know the names of our great-grandparents. There's an abiding sense that our past has shaped us in some way. Hence the growing interest in tracing family trees, TV programmes about family history, and DNA ancestry kits.

Tracing his family tree wouldn't tell Blake anything about the values and convictions of his forebears. Still, his grandmother, though not a churchgoer, had seen the change in him. She'd been treasuring some things from her father, John, and had been waiting for the right person to entrust them to. Among those things, were a couple of postcards, and a plaque that hung over John's bed all his life from the age of nine.